Jesse Owens

Olympic Star

Patricia and Fredrick McKissack

Series Consultant: Dr. Russell L. Adams, Chairman,
Department of Afro-American Studies, Howard University

Illustrated by Michael David Biegel

❖ *Great African Americans Series* ❖

ENSLOW PUBLISHERS, INC.

44 Fadem Road	P.O. Box 38
Box 699	Aldershot
Springfield, N.J. 07081	Hants GU12 6BP
U.S.A.	U.K.

To Our Friend, (Sir) Christopher Powell

Library of Congress Cataloging-in-Publication Data

McKissack, Pat, 1944-
    Jesse Owens : Olympic star / Patricia and Fredrick McKissack.
      p. cm. — (Great African Americans series)
    Includes index.
    Summary: Describes the life of the sharecroppers' son who became
an Olympic legend, and challenged Hitler's dream of Aryan
superiority.
    ISBN 0-89490-312-8
    1. Owens, Jesse, 1913-   —Juvenile literature. 2. Track and
field athletes—United States—Biography—Juvenile literature.
[1. Owens, Jesse, 1913- . 2. Track and field athletes. 3. Afro-
Americans—Biography.] I. McKissack, Fredrick. II. Title.
III. Series: McKissack, Pat, 1944- Great African Americans series.
GV697.O9M35 1992
796.42'092—dc20
[B]   92-3584
                                              CIP
                                              AC
Printed in the United States of America

10 9 8 7 6 5 4 3

Photo Credits: Library of Congress, pp. 6, 8; The Ohio State University Archives, pp. 4, 16, 21,
28.

Illustrations Credit: Michael David Biegel

Cover Illustration Credit: Ned O.

jB
OWENS

McKissack, Pat,
1944-

Jesse Owens.

$12.95

DATE			
AUG 2 9 1996			
FEB 5 1997			

BAKER & TAYLOR

Contents

1 From J.C. to Jesse 5

2 The Buckeye Bullet 11

3 The Berlin Olympics 15

4 A Good Sport 19

5 Reach for Greatness 25

Words to Know 30

Index 32

James Cleveland (Jesse) Owens
Born: September 12, 1913, Oakville, Alabama.
Died: March 31, 1980, Tucson, Arizona.

1

From J.C. to Jesse

Henry Owens was a poor farmer in Oakville, Alabama. His wife Emma washed and ironed other people's clothes for extra money. The Owens family worked very hard. But they were still poor.

Henry Owens and his family were sharecroppers. A big landowner let them grow cotton on a small piece of his land. They gave most of their cotton to the landowner to pay for the land. They sold the little bit that was left so they could buy

This is the way most sharecroppers lived in the early 1900s.

food and other things they needed. They could not save any money.

James Cleveland Owens was born in 1913. He was Henry and Emma's tenth child. They called him J.C. He was a sickly baby. His parents were afraid that he might not live.

J.C. was sick every winter. His lungs

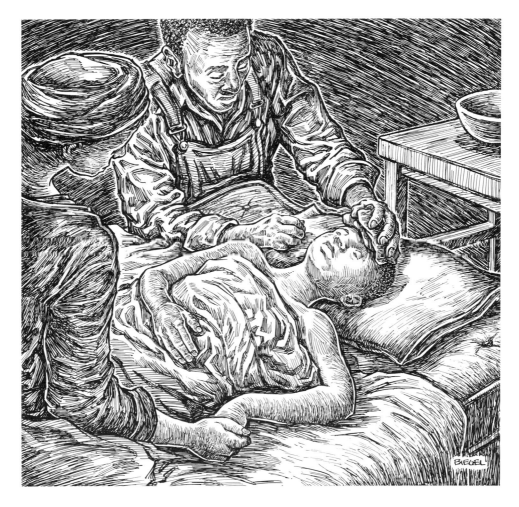

were weak. J.C.'s mother and father did
not have money to pay a doctor. They took
care of him the best way they could.

J.C.'s brothers and sisters helped their
parents with the farm. They didn't have

much time for school. They spent long hot days in the sun picking cotton. Some chopped the cotton, and some took the seeds out of the fuzzy blossoms.

J.C.'s father wanted a better life for his family. In 1921 he sold his mule. The

The Owens family did what a lot of other southern African Americans were doing at this time. They moved to Cleveland hoping for better jobs, education, and housing.

family used the money to move to Cleveland, Ohio.

Henry Owens could not find steady work in Cleveland. But J.C. could go to school. On his first day at his new school, the teacher asked J.C. what his name was. She heard him say "Jesse," not J.C. From then on, everyone called him Jesse.

2

The Buckeye Bullet

When Jesse was fourteen years old, the coach of the junior high school track team asked him to be on the team. The coach's name was Charles Riley. Every day Jesse got up early and met Coach Riley at the track.

Jesse's lungs were still bad, and he was often sick. He trained with Coach Riley every morning. Running helped Jesse's lungs, and he grew stronger. And he was even running faster.

By the time he was in high school, Jesse Owens was making a name for himself. Everybody at Cleveland East Technical High School was proud of his track records. He worked very hard to become a fast runner and a good jumper.

He ran dashes, and did high jumps and broad jumps (long jumps). And he broke national high school records almost every time he ran or jumped. Jesse was asked to come to Ohio State University and run for

the track team. But he told track coach Larry Snyder that he could not go. Jesse had to work to help his family because his father still wasn't working.

Coach Snyder wanted Jesse to run on the Ohio State team. The coach helped Henry Owens get a job as a janitor at the university. Now Jesse did not have to work to help his family. He could work to pay his own way through school.

Jesse trained harder and harder. He wanted to be the best. On May 25, 1935, Jesse broke five world records and tied another record at the University of Michigan at Ann Arbor.

Ohio State sports teams were nicknamed the Buckeyes. So after that day, people started calling Jesse "the Buckeye Bullet." He was on his way to the 1936 Olympics in Berlin, Germany.

3

The Berlin Olympics

There were 66 Americans on the 1936 Summer Olympic track and field team. Ten of them were African Americans.

Adolf Hitler, the leader of Germany, came to the games on the opening day. The large crowd cheered for him. They raised their arms and shouted "Heil Hitler!"

Hitler was a Nazi. He believed that Germans were the "master race." He said they would rule the world one day. He also said that Jews and people of color

On the first day of the Olympics, Jesse beat all the other runners in the first trial run of the 100-meter race.

were not equal to whites. Hitler hoped
these Olympics would prove he was
right.

Jesse Owens was the star of the 1936
Olympic Games. He won the 100-meter
dash. Ralph Metcalf, who was also an
African American, came in second. Then,
Jesse won the 200-meter dash. Matthew

Robinson, another black man, came in second.

Other black athletes did well too. Cornelius Johnson, David Albritton, and Delos Thurber won the gold, silver, and bronze medals in the high jump. Adolf Hitler was very upset.

4

A Good Sport

Jesse was doing very well at the Olympics. Then something went wrong in the broad jump event. People were surprised that the great Jesse Owens was in trouble. When he did his first jump, he thought it was a practice jump. But it wasn't. Now he only had two more tries. If he missed these jumps, he would not get into the final round.

Jesse got set. He did his next jump. "Scratched," the judge shouted. Jesse's foot was over the white line. The jump didn't count. He had only one more jump left. If he missed this jump, he was out.

Luz Long was a very good broad jumper. Luz was Germany's best hope for a gold medal in this event. He spoke to Jesse. His English was not very good. "I am Luz Long," he said. "You need to calm yourself." He smiled at Jesse. The two young men talked until Jesse felt calmer. Jesse's last jump was good. He would compete against Luz in the finals.

Jesse beat Luz Long in the final broad jump and set a world record. Luz surprised everyone. He raised Jesse's arm and shouted, "Jesse . . . Jesse." The crowd joined in and shouted "Jesse. . . Jesse!" People cheered for both Jesse and Luz. They were both winners.

Jesse was also part of the 400-meter

When Jesse took his final jump in the long-jump he leaped into history. He said he never wanted to come down. "I was going to stay up in the air forever." But he did come down in a record-breaking jump of 26 feet, 5⁵⁄₁₆ inches. The record would hold until 1960.

relay team. Jesse was not part of the original team. Jesse and Ralph Metcalfe replaced the two starting American runners, named Marty Glickman and Sam Stoller.

Some people believe that Glickman and Stoller were replaced because they were Jewish. They were very angry. But Glickman and Stoller still cheered when the American 400-meter relay team won first place. Jesse had won another gold medal. He went home with four gold medals.

Jesse never saw Luz Long again. Luz was killed in World War II. After the war ended, Jesse went back to Germany. He visited Luz's family. Jesse told them what Luz had done for him at the Olympics. The families became friends.

5

Reach for Greatness

Jesse had married his high school sweetheart, Ruth, in 1935. They had three daughters: Gloria, Beverly, and Marlene.

Jesse faced some tough times after the Olympics. When he first came home, Jesse was treated like a star. People offered him many business deals. Jesse tried to be fair and honest. He believed other people were fair and honest, too. He was wrong. A lot of people were not fair with Jesse. He lost a lot of money.

Jesse started some businesses that worked out well. Others failed. Jesse went back to Ohio State for a while. He was not a very good student.

Jesse enjoyed working with children. He was very good at working with kids and helping start athletic programs. He worked for the Recreation Department of

Cook County (Chicago), Illinois. He told young children all over America to, "reach for greatness."

Many people worked for the rights of African Americans during the 1960s. African Americans did win some rights, but there was still prejudice. There were still many black people who were poor. They had little hope of doing better, and African Americans were angry.

Jesse wrote a book called *Blackthink* in 1970. He said that African Americans did not get ahead because they did not want to. Many people did not like the book. They wrote angry letters to Jesse. Some letters said that Jesse was too famous to know about the prejudice against many African Americans.

Jesse read the letters carefully. He thought again about the problems of

African Americans. In 1972, he wrote another book called *I Have Changed*. In this book, he apologized for some of the things he said in *Blackthink*.

Jesse Owens was given many honors in his life. In February 1979, President

Ohio State University gave Jesse an honorary degree in 1972. He won other awards, too. In 1950 the Associated Press named him the greatest track and field athlete in history.

Jimmy Carter gave Jesse Owens an award at the White House. President Carter said, "He has always helped others to reach for greatness."

Jesse Owens died of lung cancer on March 31, 1980, in Tucson, Arizona. He was 66 years old.

Words to Know

broad jump—A track and field event now called the long jump. Athletes compete to see how far they can jump. There are two events. In one, the athletes begin from a standing position. In the other, they get a running start.

bronze medal—The award that is given to the third place winner in Olympic events.

coach—A person who helps train and guide athletes in a specific sport.

dash—A short-distance running competition.

finals—The championship competition in a sporting event.

gold medal—The award that is given to the first place winner in Olympic events.

high jump—A track and field event. Athletes compete to see who can jump the highest. The athletes jump over a high cross bar and try not to knock it off.

Heil Hitler—A Nazi cheer. It means *Hail Hitler*— or *Praises to Hitler.*

Hitler, Adolf—The Nazi leader of Germany from 1933 to 1945.

Nazi—The dominant political party in Germany from 1933 to 1945.

Olympics—A sporting event where athletes from all over the world compete for medals in all kinds of sports. The first Olympics were held in ancient Greece. The new Olympics began in 1896. They are held every four years in different countries.

prejudice—A dislike of people, places, or things without a good reason.

president—A person who is the leader of a country or a group.

silver medal—The award that is given to the second place winner in Olympic events.

track and field meet—A competition where the sports are running, jumping, and throwing.

world record—The best performance in the world of a sports event.

Index

A African Americans,
         rights of, 27
      Albritton, David, 18

B Berlin, Germany, 13
      Blackthink, 27, 28
      broad jump, 12, 19–20

C Carter, Jimmy, 28–29
      Cleveland, Ohio, 9
      Cleveland East Technical
         High School, 12

G Germany, 15, 20, 23
      Glickman, Marty, 23

H Hitler, Adolf, 15, 17, 18

I *I Have Changed*, 28

J Jews, 15
      Johnson, Cornelius, 18

L Long, Luz, 20, 23

M Metcalfe, Ralph, 17, 23

N Nazi, 15

O Oakville, Alabama, 5
      Ohio State University,
         12, 13, 26
      Olympic Games (1936),
         13, 15–23, 25
      Owens, Emma, 5
      Owens, Henry, 5, 8–9, 13
      Owens, James Cleveland
         (Jesse)
         birth of, 6

      brothers and sisters
         of, 6, 7
      called "the Buckeye
         Bullet," 13
      childhood of, 6–9
      children of, 25
      death of, 29
      joins track team, 11
      marriage of, 25
      sets world records,
         13, 20
      Owens, Ruth, 25

R Recreation Department
         of Cook County
         (Chicago),
         Illinois, 26–27
      Riley, Charles, 11
      Robinson, Matthew, 17–18

S sharecroppers, 5
      Snyder, Larry, 13
      Stoller, Sam, 23

T Thurber, Delos, 18
      Tucson, Arizona, 29

U University of Michigan at
         Ann Arbor, 13
      U.S. Olympic track team
         (1936), 15,
         17–18, 22–23

W World War II, 23